ONE MAN'S MOON

ONE MAN'S MOON

Poems by Bashō & Other Japanese Poets

Versions by Cid Corman

EXPANDED EDITION

GNOMON PRESS

FIRST EDITION

Cover photographs by DOBREE ADAMS.
FRONT: TEAHOUSE, CHUSON-JI TEMPLE AT HIRAIZUMI,
BACK: ANCIENT FOREST OF HAGURO-SAN,
BOTH SITES VISITED BY BASHŌ IN HIS
TRAVELS TO THE NORTH.

ISBN 0-917788-76-1

LIBRARY OF CONGRESS CONTROL NUMBER:
2003102045

Copyright © 1984, 1988, 1990,
1991, 1999, 2001, 2003

Published by
GNOMON PRESS
P. O. Box 475
Frankfort
KY 40602-0475

CONTENTS

ACKNOWLEDGMENTS

This expanded edition of *One Man's Moon* collects poems from many previous publications as well as translations that have never before appeared in book form. *Cool Melon* and *Cool Gong* were first published by Origin Press in 1959. The original *One Man's Moon, 50 Haiku by Bashō, Buson, Issa, Hakuin, Shiki, Santōka* appeared in 1984; *Born of a Dream, 50 Haiku by Bashō, Buson, Taigi, Issa, Shiki* appeared in 1988; *Little Enough, 50 Haiku by Bashō, Sodō, Ransetsu, Buson, Ryōkan, Issa, Shiki and a Tanka by Sōkan* appeared in 1991 — all from Gnomon Press. *Walking into the Wind, A Sweep of Poems by Santōka* was issued by Jeffrey Miller's Cadmus Editions in 1990. *A Real Issa* and *So Here You Are* (all poems by Bashō) were issued in 1999 and 2001 by John Martone's tel-let. *Being Saigyō, Japanese Buddhist Monk,* and various publications of Corman's versions of Bashō, Sengai, Issa and Ozaki Hōsai have been published though the years by Bob Arnold's Longhouse.

The publisher thanks Bob Arnold, John Martone, Jeffrey Miller, Ce Rosenow, and Eliot Weinberger, all of whom helped make this book possible.

INTRODUCTION

Haiku are Japanese poems developed from earlier short syllabic songs and fully established as a genre with the advent of Bashō (1644-94), the poet given the most play in these pages. He hewed to the 5-7-5 structure and also by and large kept to the seasonal stricture. These haiku were essentially songs composed 'on the move' rather than written at a desk. The feeling of a life being lived in relation to the natural world is central and unmistakable. Bashō's was a life devoted to poetry and the life of an itinerant Buddhist priest. His dates tell you it was relatively short and all the apparently richer for it.

> old pond
> frog leaping
> splash

This most known of haiku poems by Bashō could even be written as one word and be closer to the way the Japanese read/recite haiku. Although my version takes the original to its minimal (and exact) word for word translation – it stresses each word as syllable/sound – as well as indicating how a haiku often, like a Japanese sentence, is no more than the modifying of a noun. A word made alive by defining perception/relation.

Often the final word is an untranslatable -*kana* – an expletive not unlike Shakespeare's famous question mark with its exclamatory force. But often also scoring a sigh – the enduring barely endurable transience of being alive.

The poets represented here are the major exponents of the form – which has tended to be so overused as to have lost most of its chance of greater extension.

Hakuin (1686-1769) is best known as the founder of modern (Rinzai) Zen and for his calligraphic art. The particular poem of his here is one written on a painting of his I've lived with for 25 years and one he wrote in his late 20's at a temple near Ōsaka and from which his own name (White Sound) was derived.

Buson (1716-83), painter and poet, and Issa (1763-1827), poet and itinerant priest, are regarded as Bashō's major successors. Issa's life was of an unendurable and incredible wretchedness – sorrow piled upon sorrow on the face of it – and yet out of the depths of it or in it the poetry finds its precarious crucial security, its ounce of joy, its thimbleful of delight.

Shiki (1867-1902) is usually thought of as the key figure in launching a modern haiku movement, but always you can feel his relation of the traditional.

Santōka (1882-1940) is the last in the great line of itinerant monks – Bashō, Issa, and Ryōkan the others in mind. Santōka, as chance had it, discovered or was brought to the practice and discipline of Soto Zen as a dispensation that connected with poetry, at the very moment life itself had lost meaning for him (suicide only just averted).

His poems worked more openly and broke away from exact syllabic count, but made each syllable count.

It is rare enough – in any form – that anyone today finds poetry a way of 'staying alive,' yet that is what it is, if it has any validity at all.

And so it is they also still live with us. You can feel – if you let each syllable grow into – every moment of life comes to be shared – at depth.

This is what it is – not about – but is.

CID CORMAN

Saigyō

[1118-1190]

Every morning
nothing more of the leaves heard –
the wind is voiceless –
as if the night had spoken
and the heart of man had stopped.

Getting off the road
near a stream running by in
to willow shadow
for a while at any rate
and staying just a while yet.

Nowhere more to go
only to live and only
no matter where –
every straw coming home
to each in this dying world.

That's the way it is
and had to be – despite thought –
froze bamboo water
pipe – something to think about –
the spring being awaited.

With snow fallen on
field paths and mountain paths too
covering them up
who knows where anything is –
all goings up in the air.

You are so nicely
into the weave you wear and
beyond undoing –
ah to be woven with
you – to have become that close.

With every spring
the blossoms offered heart/mind
their consolation
for more than years can ever
say of what keeps going on.

The sound of the waves
comes dashing over mind/heart
all night long alas
the rushmatted roof lets moon
light leak through at the same time.

Within this world the
people tend to disappear
going as they go
and the thought realized makes
anybody look foolish.

Still being absorbed
in the surge of the blossoms
when they were going –
at their peak so much white cloud
cascading all the way down.

Yoshinoyama
ok aware of you I
surely will be key
to your blossoms profoundly
entered into already.

A long way off here
rock of a gorge surrounding
being quite alone
and out of sight of others
to think everything through.

Sōkan

[1458-1546]

If anyone asks
where Sōkan has gone you can –
quite properly – say
he's off on his usual
mission – wherever it takes.

Sōkan was something of a model for
Bashō in the wake of Saigyō. Sometimes
regarded as the inventor of renga.
This tanka at the approach of death.

Bashō

[1644-1694]

With odor of plum
bursts the sunrise
mountain path.

Morning-dewed
streaked cool
muddy melon.

With the sparrow chicks
all the peeping to each other
a nestful of mice.

Azaleas
   stuck in a bucket
woman
ripping dried cod.

This is winter's day
upon a horse frozen stiff
a monkish shadow.

Touring the world
tilling a small field
to its limits.

All the day long
insatiably brimming
the lark.

Departing spring (ya
the birds at their cries fishes'
eyes Amida tears.

Amida (the nembutsu prayer : Buddha invoked)

How inspiriting
the green leaves young leaves of a
sun's resplendency.

Only for a time
to a waterfall confined
summer opening.

Across the meadow
horse take your lead now from the
hototogisu.

This bird is the cuckoo but the Japanese
is reflective of the sound to Japanese ears.

Natural grace's
beginning found in Oku's
rice-planting singing.

Furyu (wind-fluent) is an esthetic term and this
is its *locus classicus*. Oku is the backland north
and west of Tokyo.

The summer grasses
the mightiest warriors'
dreams' consequences.

What with fleas and lice
the horse having a good piss
right at the pillow.

Silence itself is
in the rock saturated
are cicada sounds.

Rough as the sea is
reaching over to Sado
the Heaven's star stream.

Sado is the famed island of old exile
off the west coast of Honshu.
The 'star stream' is the Milky Way.

The rains of summer
gathering rapidly to
Mogamigawa.

-gawa is river; in Honshu

Tomb you also move
my own voice's lamenting
the autumnal winds.

The autumn coolness
hand and hand paring away
eggplant cucumber.

Scarlet on scarlet
the sun unrelentingly
the autumn winds.

Merciless indeed
under the ancient helmet
a cricket crickets.

Night all of that night
the autumn winds being heard
beyond the mountains.

This was after his companion (Sora) – ill –
had to leave him amidst a long walking trip.

Sweeping the garden
but letting the temple keep
the willows' droppings.

Old pond
frog leaping
splash.

Born of a dream
what can we know
  of the real?

      Neither here nor there
      unbegun unended
      wake of a bird
        erasing direction.

        A hurried moon
        treetops fastened by
        rain.

Grass for a pillow
devotion's flower-viewing
coming home to life.

        I eat my morning rice.
        I see the morning glories.

Uguisi ya
in the small bamboo thicket
singing of old age.

The *uguisi* – the bush warbler – is the shy
harbinger of spring whose call notes the name registers.
See pages 25, 42, 69, 83.

The spring and the rain
coming down through the wasps' nest
a leak in the roof.

Sun the direction
the hollyhocks incline to
in the late spring rain.

On the horse dozing
mind unsettled moon remote
tea from signs of smoke.

Without a *kasa*
myself and the cold downpour
what's it all about.

The *kasa*, the familiar peaked hat
field hands and wandering monks wore.

At cock
crow cold rain at
the cow shed.

Rain rain rain enough
to turn all the stubble to
black black black enough.

Polishing up the
mirror to be as clear as
the flowers of snow.

Extracting gray hairs
from under the pillow
a cricket.

That on the Buddha's
birthday should be born
a fawn.

The salted bream's
bums are also icy cold
fishmonger's counter.

Autumn aching close
the heart more given to the
four-and-a-half mats.

4½ tatami space is that of
the ideal tearoom and taken
as the space of love.

The leeks so white
from having just been washed
coldness itself.

Somehow still not dead
tho the journey's at its end
autumn darkening.

The years first snow
building upon the building
up on the bridge.

Honk of snot
blown into the open hand
plum blossom supreme.

A springtide evening
a single figure haunting
the temple's corner.

At Hasedera [Nara] – a favorite place
for women seeking Kwannon's compassion.

Spring if here indeed
with no name for the hill in-
to its morning mists.

Whatever the tree
flowering may be it is
none the less fragrant.

The greening willows
splattering about the mud
with the tide gone out.

Cherry blossom clouds –
is the temple bell Ueno
or Asakusa?

These favorite Edo locales – equally so
in spring in postmodern Tokyo.

Uguisu there
beyond the line of willows
before the thickets.

See page 20.

See page 20.

At every gust
the butterfly resettles
for a willow leaf.

Sick and tired of kids –
words of somebody who's gone
and lost his flowers.

In the summer rains
one unhideable object
Seta O-hashi.

Famed bridge for viewing just south
of Lake Biwa at Kusatsu.

Both hills and garden
are making their move upon
summer's drawing room.

One piece taken off
only to tote on the back
changing apparel.

Into summer robes
and even the lice haven't
got the message yet.

On a bare branch a
crow finally gets a grip
fall night coming on.

Out in the cow-shed
mosquito hummings feeble
autumn has its winds.

A plenary moon
the priest's children all lined up
on the temple porch.

Today is the time –
folks – getting old gets to feel
a first wintry blast.

Autumn getting on
wishing to get at last to
Little Pine River.

A full harvest moon
coming to this very gate
the tide its highest.

A frond of plantain
should be hung on the doorpost
a hut for the moon.

Bashō – the word means plantain.

A crescent moon and
the earth turning hazier
buckwheat flowering.

Hototogisu
warbling some five feet over
the blue irises.

See page 15.

Both hands chock full of
peach and cherry blossoms and
mugwort rice cakes too.

The cats making love
once they've stopped in the bedroom
a faint vernal moon.

In any event
nothing worse in the snow than
withered miscanthus.

In cold wintry wind
some fragrance has caught onto
returning flowers.

GREETING BAIJIN (1691)

The narcissuses
and white paper sliding doors
harmonize nicely.

MENSHOJI

A century al-
ready seen in the garden's
fallen leaves right now.

Under the noodles
getting the kindling going
a cold night indeed!

From time to time some
vinegared chrysanthemums
to spike the *saké*.

SANSHI

Seeing buckwheat too
making me feel jealous of
the bushclover field.

Rice being finished
friends over this evening to keep
the moon company.

In the cattle shed
mosquitoes teasing darkness
summer heat something.

Preparing dumplings
with one hand she pushes back
a dangling forelock.　　　·

SO
HERE
YOU
ARE

This one time it's
Bashō having you along
to wave goodbye to.

Up on a dead bough
a crow has come to settle
this autumn evening.

Plantain wind-shaken
in the stone basin the rain
being heard all night.

See page 28.

Weatherbeaten fields
at heart/mind the winds into
getting into life.

END OF FALL

Misty wet weather
making Fuji hard to see
interestingly.

On horseback nodding
half-a-dream the moon way off
tea steaming away.

Monks – morning glories –
often returning to die –
the nature of plants.

The dew drops dripping
as if wanting to – trying
to clean up this world.

Gravely gravelly
the sound of the hailstones on
this *hinoki* hat.

hinoki : hat monks wear made
of strips of this sacred cypress

MOVING
ON

The year has ended –
straw hat on and straw sandals
snuggled right into.

LATE
FEBRUARY

Is it really spring –
even the nameless hills re-
tain a veil of mist

Right now together
let's get some brown rice as grub
and share a grass bed.

Summer clothing from
which all the lice have yet to
be all extracted.

Clouds now and again
giving folks a respite from
all this moon-viewing.

ASAKUSA

The Kuanon Temple
tiled roof sighted now amidst
cherry blossom clouds.

Asakusa – famed cherry blossom
locale in Tokyo. *See p. 25.*

Mountain path to come
upon so beautifully
a wild violet.

Just one possession
in this world of mine and light –
nothing but a gourd.

First snow of the year
the leaves of the daffodils
bowing to the scene.

After the *saké*
harder and harder to sleep
tonight with the snow.

Finding no one home –
even the plum blossoms on
a neighboring fence.

High over the field
with not a thing to cling to
a skylark warbling.

SUMMERY

Now indeed has the
proper clothing been put on –
cicada costume.

The poor farmer child
even while hulling the rice
looking to the moon.

Pine pins being burnt
a hand towel being dried
cold is cold indeed.

To the tune of
the skylarks the beat of
the pheasant.

LUMBAGO

Medicine to take
even without the frost on
the pillow alas.

Home country once more
umbilicus drawing tears
the year at its end.

A family custom then to keep
umbilical cords as tokens.

Whimsicality?
On a scentless blade of grass
a butterfly perched.

A *saké* cup is
no place to drop your shit in –
you bunch of swallows.

Paper apparel
getting wet in garnering
the rained-on blossoms.

So many many
memories are brought to mind
with cherry blossoms.

More than any lark
in the sky to be resting
in a mountain pass!

Were this voice a voice
there would be a song to sing
of blossoms falling.

Using a fresh leaf
with eyesight filling with tears
to wipe them away.

All tuckered out and
taking lodgings at an inn
wisteria flowers.

Nothing hidden here
this house with its soup of greens
and its red pepper.

1689

First winter shower
monkey too a short raincoat
seems to be wanting.

Right now children how
about a real romp in the
humdinger hailstones?

TŌDAIJI

First snow already –
when is the Great Buddha to
have his temple built?

What in the world at
this year end's market is the
crow out flying for?

An *uguisu's*
head covering has been dropt
– camellia petal!

See page 20.

Are you butterfly
and am I the famed Chuang Tzu –
O dream of heart/mind?

Firefly viewing time
and the boatman getting drunk
undependable.

This is my place and
a little mosquito
the entertainment.

Pretty soon to die
but no sign is visible
cicada soundings.

Winter seclusion
again leaning up against
this selfsame pillar.

Both of us have seen
snow indeed this year and, man,
has it been falling!

Hackberries falling
starlings wingbeating around
rough morning weather.

Should something be said
when lips are found shivering
autumn has its gusts.

Must borrow for sleep
a scarecrow's kimono – ay –
given midnight's frost.

The horse keeps going
like one astride a painting
dead of winter field.

Fire under the ash
and written on the wall the
shadow of a friend.

Nothing
lasts forever.

That's the trouble
with it.

Fall deepening in
– how are the neighbors and how
are they making out?

Nearing his own death.

Hard going way worn
dreaming of waste after waste
going on and on.

Bashō's famous last poem.

Sodō

[1643-1716]

A house for the spring
there is nothing more here but
whatever is is

Ransetsu

[1654-1707]

One plum blossom more
and that very one more is
where the warmth comes in.

Hakuin

[1686-1769]

So others also
hear in Shinoda fields at
temple twilight snow.

Shinoda – near Osaka.

Taigi

[1709-1771]

The first flush of love
up against a stone lantern
a face and a face.

A robber no less
run across by a fox
in a melon patch.

Coming on quickly
back and forth swarms already
what else but swallows.

The heart gets too much
the peony bending in
a matter of days.

A sudden downpour
unimaginable sound
upon the forest.

Don't break it off – but
broken given concluded
a garden of plums.

cf. William Carlos Williams'
famous poem, 'The Act'

Fugu for supper
the man even now sleeping
mumbles his prayers.

Fugu – the globefish famed
for its poisonous innards, with
which some foolhardy natives
in their cups like to get a buzz
on with – sometimes to their
own demise.

The porch's edge is
all wet and that's about it –
autumn has its rain.

The opening word (composed
of two kanji) embana: literally
reads – 'karma edge'

So each so many
stars making their appearance
and the cold cold still.

Buson

[1716-1783]

How salutary
to rip some bibs of paper
off the gods of rock.

Many temples have tiny *jizō* statues along
their edge – wearing bibs (of paper often), good
luck figures, deity of children and pregnant women.

The one adornment
of an alien homestead
spring's earliest mist.

At the mountain's foot
the rice being planted sounds
wisteria blooms.

A mountain temple
bungled being struck on the
bell getting hazy.

The great gateway with
its great and heavy portals
and the spring twilight.

Swallowing clouds and
hawking up cherry blossoms
Yoshino-yama.

One of the famous cherry viewing sites;
yama: mountain.

How slow the days are
echoings remembering
Kyoto neighborhoods.

Bashō went away
and ever since that day now
the year never ends.

Lost in a hot tub
looking down upon my legs
this morning this fall.

Take it easy – fool –
window darkening – says the
snowed-upon bamboo.

The clearest of dews
on the thorns of the bushes
a single drop each.

Uguisu ya
the family completed
food for everyone.

See page 20.

Light of one candle
used in lighting another
on this spring evening.

A summer river
and crossing it happiness
with sandals in hand.

One man is coming
one man is making a call
fall night coming on.

Sengai

[1750-1837]

Crown of grid iron –
there's nothing to think about –
only all to use.

Over Everest
the same old moon shares its light
as clear as ever
but only for eyes ready
to see the darkness clearer.

Moon empty
sky shine
water deepened
darkness.

Forget alone and
forget you have forgotten—
have it both your ways.

Yes or no –
good or bad –
you have come

to this house.
Here is your
tea – your cake.

Wind sweeping
the willow
and willow

the wind but
neither can
be brushed off.

Just resting –
letting the
breezes make

a thing of
a body.

Ryōkan

[1758-1831]

Scouring the pot
sound of it confusing with
that of a tree frog.

All is for kindling
the winds out there collecting
all the fallen leaves.

The robber had been
but had somehow left behind
the wide window's moon.

Lost in a dream world
and once again the dream ends
grass for a pillow
awakening all alone
having to think of it too.

Issa

[1763-1827]

Only one guy and
only one fly trying to
make the guest room do.

Pee-pul
upright scarecrows also
scarce.

Mosquitoes pests but
without them it'd be a lot
lonelier yet.

The old man's day and
saying something about it
the front door sparrows.

The old man here is Bashō:
presumably his birthday.

Shut up – cicada
now that Mister Whiskers has
got into the act.

In the world of men
into the field being worked
the lotus flowers.

Unless you're here
honestly there's more than
enough trees.

To go from one hot
tub to soak in another
so much silliness.

A change of clothing
but coming along for the
ride the selfsame lice.

Uguisu ya
wiping its muddy feet
the plum blossoms.

See pages 20.

Come on – sparrow – hey
it's against the law to shit
on the old bedding.

There's the old cricket
lifting up its whiskers to
make its insect sound.

The very first sky
now being manufactured
out of the first smoke.

This would not be tobacco but the hearth.

At the altarplace
nammu nammu all that a
little child can say.

The child's attempt at saying namu-amida-
butsu (the usual short prayer repeated).

The New Year's presents
held by mother the child too
holding out its hands.

The snow is melting
the village is brimming with
all at once children.

Congratulations
are just about in order –
this is my spring time.

On New Year's Day too
everything just the same –
the house a shambles.

Spring is beginning –
folly once again upon
folly returning.

Swinging from the tree
a spring of cherry blossoms
being clung to yet.

The bell sound fading
the scent of blossoms ringing
evening even yet.

Having put to bed
the child there's the laundry now
and a summer moon.

With years coming on
even the length of a day's
enough to draw tears.

This is peacefulness –
Asama issuing smoke
and a midday moon.

Mt. Asama – at the edge of Nagano/Gumma
Prefectures – still active NW of Tokyo.

A hazy day the
emptiness quieter ac-
commodating room.

The mountainous moon
on the one stealing flowers
bestows more splendor.

Hurry-scurry a
butterfly out for the day
eye still on the till.

Looking straight at me
making a terrible face
nothing but a frog.

All's well with the world
another mouth is welcome
at the rice bowl – fly.

The cicada's call
exactly the same red as
that of the pinwheel.

The sleeping dog is
covered enough in passing
by a single leaf.

Were my father here
at dawn we'd be out looking
at the green rice fields.

On New Year's Day to
be becoming a child – yes
visibly again.

Hey little sparrow
better get out of the way –
a horse is coming.

Morning glories
enough thatch
for this hut.

Here at the old hut
grass worn by summer too has
what it gets to take.

That's a big rock there –
look out for your noggins you
flittering fireflies.

Ants getting along
from the cloud summits down to
as far as they can.

A dewdrop world ay
a dewdrop world but even
so – but even so.

Shiki

[1867-1902]

Despite icy winds
a temple bell abandoned
along the way.

The boat and the shore
conversing all day long in
terms of the water.

One falls and all at
once a second has fallen –
camellias like that.

A short night it is –
the vastness of a beach with
its discarded broom.

A long night it is –
but just beyond the *shōji*
a light's going by.

shōji: the sliding paper door wall

Santōka

[1882-1940]

Alone but
the mosquitoes
won't let me be.

With all this rain
the birds have
nothing to eat.

The mountains'
silence be
comes the rain's.

Working at it and
working at it and still
the tall grass grows.

Going back
one man's moon
and the one way.

Finally clearing
I too can get back today
to the wash.

Opening the window
a window full
of spring.

Mountains darkening
mountain voices
being heard.

Sticky-hot
living things
living things become.

Picking and offering
an unknown flower
to Lord Buddha.

So many dry twigs
snapping snapping
thinking nothing now.

No *saké* now
only the moon there
to be stared at.

Having some rice
having some books and
even having tobacco.

Just wanting to walk
walking with a beggar's bag
plump full evening moon.

Chilly
the clouds
in a rush.

Passersby passers
by and coming
together going.

Belly full
drinking water
bringing on sleep.

Cherry blossoms
in full bloom
imprisoning.

From the hills a breeze
reaching a windbell thinking
of wanting to live.

The waves sound sometimes
close and sometimes far away
how much more of life.

Sometimes the begging
stops for the mountains
want looking at.

On the *kasa* a
dragonfly has settled
for a walk.

See page 21.

A great spot to stay
every which way mountains and
a *saké* shop in front.

The horse
trampling upon
the grass the
flowers blossoming.

Scanty subsistence
even the water is
running away.

Exhilarating
letting the temple bell get
a bang out of it.

Santōka as a belated novice at the
Mitori Kannon-do (outskirts of Kumamoto,
Japan Sea side of Kyushu) would ring the
bell each sunrise and sundown as
one of his duties.

Snow light brightness
the house completely
quietness.

From the mountains
white flowers
at the desk.

That was my very
own face there in the mirror
shivering cold.

The surviving flies
would seem to have
remembered me.

Getting old
face to face
saying nothing.

Completely pointless
Hōtei now but
still smiling away.

Hōtei: a wooden figure of the old
potbellied bald good luck god
(from China & Korea).

Looking down on
the sleeping village below
and pissing away.

If it's fair it bleats,
if it's cloudy it bleats,
a goat—the one goat.

Men women
and the shadows too
dancing.

Down to the skin the
bath-house conversation's
picking up steam.

Moneyless
thingless toothless
alone.

Of my birthplace
there are no more traces
fireflies.

The evening's
loneliness
again the garden
to water.

The waves' sounds
drenching
darkness.

A lovely path
to a lovely building
the charnel house.

Hōsai

[1885-1926]

Without a bowl
both hands
receiving.

In the nail box
all the nails
bent.

ABOUT THE TRANSLATOR

CID CORMAN was born in Boston in 1924 and educated at Boston Latin School and Tufts College, with post-graduate work at the University of Michigan, University of North Carolina, and the Sorbonne. He founded the magazine and press *Origin* in 1951, publishing many of the major poets of the twentieth century including William Carlos Williams, Wallace Stevens, Louis Zukofsky, Lorine Niedecker, Charles Olson, Gary Snyder, Robert Duncan, Denise Levertov, William Bronk, and Robert Creeley.

He is the author of countless books of poems, including the five-volume *Of* (three volumes published so far). Corman has also published translations from French, German, Italian, Japanese, and other languages. He has lived mainly out of the United States, first in Europe and now for most of the past forty-five years in Kyoto, Japan. From the Japanese he has also translated Bashō's *Back Roads to Far Towns* and collections of the work of Kusano Shimpei and Santōka.

ABOUT THE BOOK

This book has been typeset in
Trump Mediaeval, designed by
Georg Trump, for text and
Albertus, designed by
Berthold Wolpe, for display.

Printed and bound by
Thomson-Shore, Inc.
in an edition of
1,000 copies.